This Journal Belongs To:

everyday matters
Journal

Everyday Matters Journal
Hendrickson Publishers Marketing, LLC
P. O. Box 3473
Peabody, Massachusetts 01961-3473

ISBN 978-1-61970-024-6

All rights reserved. No part of this book may be reproduced or transmitted in any form or by any means, electronic or mechanical, including photocopying, recording, or by any information storage and retrieval system, without permission in writing from the publisher.

Printed in China

First Hendrickson Edition Printing — March 2013

Scripture quotations are taken from the *Holy Bible,* New Living Translation, copyright © 1996, 2004, 2007 by Tyndale House Foundation. Used by permission of Tyndale House Publishers, Inc., Wheaton, Illinois 60189. All rights reserved.

Everyday Matters Journal

More and more Christian women are discovering the traditional spiritual disciplines and incorporating them into their daily lives. These disciplines include studying Scripture and prayer, but that is just the starting point. There's acceptance of one's self and God's personal call. There's celebration and gratitude, service and a concern for justice, dedicated times of rest and solitude, life in Christian community and worship.

This journal allows you to track your spiritual journey as it relates to twenty-four spiritual disciplines or practices. Each section features insightful quotations illuminating a specific practice that can help you shut out the distractions and busyness that hinder our awareness of God's presence with us every moment of every day.

This journal is designed to complement the *Everyday Matters Bible for Women*. There, supplementing the Bible text, you'll find more than three hundred instructional and inspirational writings by thoughtful contemporary authors. By sharing their insights—related to these twenty-four spiritual disciplines—these writers become like companions, showing you that you are not alone on your spiritual journey toward holiness and a God-honoring character.

Used alone or alongside the *Everyday Matters Bible for Women*, this journal gives you a place to record your heartfelt desires, your victories and regrets, your conversations and prayers, details of your hunger for God and God's faithful provision. Here you can note insights gleaned from your personal or group Bible study.

Of course this journal can also serve as a record of your more mundane everyday matters. The pages are yours, to fill as you see fit. Whether you write or doodle or paste in pictures, just keep in mind the reality of God's presence—with you today. Tomorrow. Every day. That's what matters.

The Spiritual Disciplines

This journal is designed to encourage the reader to focus on twenty-four of the essential practices of Christian spiritual formation. Each spiritual discipline or practice is decorated with its own distinctive icon, described here in this alphabetical summary. They are presented in the same order within the journal.

Acceptance. We may be wives, mothers, friends, physicians, or teachers. Those are all roles we play. But they are not who we are at our core. At our core, we are children of God, created in his image, called and designed with special gifts, loved intensely and unconditionally "just because." God isn't as concerned with what we do as much as with who we are. Accepting that understanding is the first step to the freedom of living out God's call on our lives.

Bible Study and Meditation. We have amazing power and strength at our fingertips through understanding and applying God's Word to our lives. This discipline looks at the prayerful deliberation of and digging in to the Scriptures in more than just a cursory read.

Celebration. The writer of Hebrews tells us that Christ was anointed with the oil of joy. One of the ways Jesus drew others to him was his unreserved ability to celebrate, play, and rejoice in all things—including finding deep abiding joy in the moments of sorrow. Through this discipline, we too learn to live with unreserved delight and joy, to play, and to have a childlike exuberance and enjoyment of life, our world, and God's goodness.

Community. God created us to live out our faith within the context of the body of Christ. The Christian life is not meant to be journeyed alone. So through this discipline we learn to engage other believers through the common practices of worship, service, prayer, celebration, confession, and other activities with the shared goal of knowing and experiencing the triune God in a fuller, more complete way.

Confession. Repentance does not stop at the prayer of salvation; it is a continual honing and shaping of our character. Confession is bringing to light those things that keep us from experiencing the fullness of our relationship with God. We also practice repentance toward God and others by confessing our weaknesses and failures in order to receive forgiveness, mercy, restoration, and healing.

Contemplation. In a rush, rush world, our minds can become so filled with clutter that we lose the ability to focus on the eternal. The practice of contemplation allows us to have deliberate, prayerful reflection on God, his will, his world, and his works.

Faith. While God blesses us with a measure of faith, we must stretch and use it. The spiritual practice of growing our faith includes moving beyond and nurturing the expectations that God plants within us; it is about actively pursuing hope and a willingness to believe.

Fasting. Many of us think about fasting in terms of giving up food every once in a while when we're in a crisis. Yet biblical characters and our church mothers and fathers discovered a great power by fasting regularly. Here we look at fasting in terms of voluntarily denying or abstaining from a need, want, or desire (food, television, the Internet, etc.) to focus more clearly and intensely on connecting with God in a deeper, more profound way.

Forgiveness. Jesus was clear with his followers when he said if we want to be forgiven, we must forgive. Too often we focus on the pain of forgiving those who have hurt us. Yet that is only part of this practice. In this discipline we look at voluntarily receiving absolution from God, others, and ourselves, and releasing the same to others *and* ourselves.

Gratitude. How great is God's love and goodness toward us! As we realize more and more just who God is and what he thinks of us, his children, our hearts overflow with gratitude. This spiritual practice is about being more intentional in our thanksgiving than just a simple, "Thanks, God." It is about reflecting and offering a *deep* thankfulness for God's goodness and workings in our lives. Gratitude often reaps celebration.

Hospitality. Throughout the Bible, God commands us over and over to take notice of and care for those around us. More than just opening our homes to our friends or Bible study group for coffee, hospitality is a conscientious pursuit to welcome strangers and friends into our homes *and lives* and to make them feel loved and accepted.

Justice. God's heart is about seeking justice for those who have been wronged. As followers, then, our hearts also break, prompting us to become intentional about seeking and pursuing advocacy on behalf of those who have been mistreated.

Mentoring. We all have experiences that have helped us grow and given us wisdom. But their benefits are diminished if we do not share what we have learned. And how much insight we can gain as we seek wisdom from others who have traveled the road before us. From Naomi and Ruth to Mary and Elizabeth, we see models of mentoring throughout the Bible. In this practice we discover the importance of receiving and giving biblical, godly wisdom and insight in order to strengthen the body of Christ.

Outreach. Jesus told us to go into the world and share the gospel. So through this spiritual practice we model and testify to those outside the Christian faith, to introduce them to Jesus and the kingdom of God.

Prayer. It's easy to think that prayer is a mode of communication in which we talk, God listens, and then does what we desire! Prayer is much deeper and complex than that. It is a two-way connection and interaction between God and us. Prayer's multifaceted forms range from simple dialogue to deep intercession on behalf of others. It pursues the understanding of where God is working and how we can come alongside him in his work.

Reconciliation. Beyond confession and forgiveness, reconciliation is about pursuing peace on behalf of God's kingdom. It includes reconciling ourselves, others within the body of Christ, and those outside the body—in particular racial, ethnic, gender, and cultural reconnection. Reconciliation allows us to experience the unity that Jesus prayed about when he asked the Father to make his disciples one; it also refers to the reconciliation we have with God.

Sabbath and Rest. Even Jesus knew the importance of resting from activity and service. Some downtime can refresh us daily, allowing time for spiritual rejuvenation. Here we also practice the freedom of the fourth commandment, in which we observe a day that includes no work, a focus on God, and enjoying the want-tos.

Service. We honor God and others by making a difference in someone's life through thoughtful and loving help, advocacy, and compassion. Service is going beyond oneself to act for the good of others and to promote the work and heart of God in our communities and around the world.

Silence. Our world and lives are so noisy! In fact the noisier they are, the more difficult it is to hear the soft whisper of the Holy Spirit speaking into our lives. So we practice periods of quiet, in which we open ourselves to hearing what God is saying to us. When we close our minds to the distractions and sounds of life we can better hear God.

Simplicity. A traditional Shaker hymn says, "'Tis a gift to be simple, 'tis a gift to be free." Living out the spiritual practice of simplicity allows us to let go of anything that clutters our lives, minds, and souls, to pursue a single-minded focus on God. It includes pursuing modesty, humility, and unpretentiousness, and releasing our desire for status, comfort, and pride.

Solitude. While community is important and has a place, we also need to have solitary time with the Creator and Lover of our souls. Solitude is also closely connected to silence. It is removing oneself from all distractions or interactions with other people, to focus solely on God.

Stewardship. Proper management is one of the first responsibilities God called us to. In the Garden of Eden, God gave Adam and Eve control of the earth and everything in it, to be good stewards. Through this practice we take care of the things God has given us to manage—including time, money, creation, and relationships—in a way that honors him and his creation.

Submission. In our me-first culture it is difficult to move against that system and put others' needs before our own wants. Yet we follow a Savior who said, "Not my will, but yours, God." The daily act of submission means we continually refine an attitude of "yes, Lord," in our relationship with him and with others. We sacrifice our need to be in control and allow ourselves to be placed under the wisdom of those who will mentor and challenge us and nurture our growth.

Worship. One of the highest offerings we can give is pure worship. Through this practice we give ourselves fully over to the adoration of the greatness and glory of almighty God.

Evaluating the Meaning of Your Spiritual Journey

Journaling, the act of writing what we observe, think, or feel, slows us down and nudges us to evaluate the meaning of our lives.

The roots of words offer us a rich source of understanding. Think of the word *contemplate.* *Templari,* its Latin root, means *space*, from which we get our word *temple*—a space carved out for God. With the prefix *con-*, the word could be paraphrased as "intensive space" or inner space. That's what you cultivate when you contemplate.

The words *diary* and *journal* spring from the Latin root *die* and the French root *jour,* both of which mean *day*. I like to connect journaling with journeying—the distance you travel in one day. Journaling can be a record of your spiritual traveling, your personal edging toward God.

Spiritually reflective writing involves *re-reflecting,* bending back, or looking back into ourselves in self-examination. For the Christian this essentially means listening for God's voice. When we become sensitive to it, to catch it with our inner ears, self-examination goes on to hear what God is saying.

Mary, Jesus' mother, is an example of this type of contemplation. Scripture tells us that she responded to her pregnancy and Jesus' early life by treasuring the moments and pondering them in her heart (Luke 2:19, 51). Even though she was probably illiterate like most Jewish teenage girls of her time, Mary had the reflective heart of a journaler—she observed, treasured, and pondered what she saw and heard. We too can open our hearts and minds and listen to God as Mary did. And if we're to learn more about ourselves as God sees us, and remember what we've learned, it will help us to write it down.

—Luci Shaw

Whatever stage you're in, trust God with this season of your life; accept its limits, but also relish its joys.

—*Kay Warren*

> *I love the way God takes any willing Christian—no matter how broken or scarred her past—and weaves every thread of her life into his kingdom-building plan!*
>
> —Katie Brazelton

> *God's calling for your life goes way beyond what you do. It's who you are, where you belong, who and how you love.*
> —Nancy Ortberg

> *You are God's image-bearer! It is not possible for you to live an insignificant life.*
>
> —Carolyn Custis James

> *I have a small notebook in which I record all the Scripture passages I want to memorize. Some of them I've already committed to memory, others I'm working on, and some I'm revisiting because I need to refresh my memory.*
>
> —*Kay Marshall Strom*

You can say to God: I can't make myself want to do what you're asking me to do right now. Create a passion in me for your Word and your ways; that's what I desire.

—**Priscilla Shirer**

> *When we eat physically, we become satisfied; when we eat spiritually, we become more hungry. Also, when we don't eat physically, we become hungry; when we don't eat spiritually, we lose our appetite.*
>
> —Cynthia Heald

> *When we come to the Word, we come to a dynamic text—alive, working in us through the Holy Spirit, speaking to us and engaging with our lives.*
>
> —**Kelli B. Trujillo**

As we celebrate God's goodness and enjoy his presence, we're empowered to hold tight to that goodness during dark times. When temptation, doubt, or loneliness assails us, our faith is strong enough to stand the test.

—George Rehberg

Through our celebration of holidays and everyday blessings, we can . . . consciously choose to recall, over and over, who God is and all he's done for us. We can affirm, Yes, this is who I am, *and,* yes, this is what I believe.

—L. L. Barkat

When all else fades from view, we see with a new clarity that the ultimate source of our happiness and delight is Christ himself.

—Wendy Murray

Celebration

As we laugh, smile, eat, and make merry with friends and family, we celebrate the goodness of God expressed through the gift of the people we love.

—Kelli B. Trujillo

Community on the Fringe

Community

Of all the spiritual disciplines, community building is the most difficult for me. Maybe it's because I've been burned one too many times by Christians. Sometimes it's their "well-meaning," but ignorant, comments. Sometimes it's their mean-spirited words and actions. So I've learned the art of community on the fringe. I show up, do my part, but never really allow myself to become too vulnerable—because I just don't want to get hurt anymore. And you can't get hurt when you aren't too invested.

I know other women who feel the same way. Their motto is that old saying, "Burn me once, shame on you. Burn me twice, shame on me." And that's how they practice living in community. On the fringe, never allowing life to get too messy—because that's too painful and takes too much energy—especially for introverted, people-pleasing, avoid-conflict-at-all-costs women. Like me.

But while it's safe, I've found that practicing community on the fringe leaves me lonely and missing the joy of growing through conflict, of being stretched, challenged, and encouraged.

Jesus did community really well—which is amazing considering the men and women who continually did and said ignorant and hurtful things to him. But he kept diving in wholeheartedly—frustrated sometimes, definitely. But always centering his life and faith in the midst of other believers. And if Christ could do it and calls me to follow him, then I guess community on the fringe isn't all that God honoring after all.

In the times when it's easiest to withdraw from those who hurt us in community, maybe God is calling us to push in deeper, to become more invested—and to find the healing from the same source as the pain.

—*Ginger Kolbaba*

> *Practicing the discipline of community means we equip one another to engage in church ministry and local service because we're motivated by real encounters with the living God.*
>
> —Hollie Baker-Lutz

The body of Christ is beautiful when we all help one another be the eyes and feet and hands of the One we follow.

—John Ortberg

The enemy wants to keep Christians isolated and hates when we bless and strengthen one another. God rejoices when we do.
—*Elaine Creasman*

To truly live in harmony means our differences must play together nicely. In music this means notes need intervals—space in between them. In life this means we give one another space too.

—*Caryn Rivadeneira*

> *Healthy repentance is vigorous and clear minded, while despair is debilitating and in fact sinful.*
>
> —*Frederica Mathewes-Green*

> *Invite God to give you a sensitive conscience and a fresh love for the things that please and delight him. Holy living is demanding, but its rewards are precious.*
>
> —*Joni Eareckson Tada*

Confession

Confession doesn't ever get easier, but it does become more natural as we begin to experience the fullness of God's forgiveness and grace.

—*Anne Jackson*

> *Guilt serves its designed purpose only if it presses us toward the God who promises forgiveness and restoration. Guilt is only a symptom; we listen to it because it drives us toward the cure.*
>
> —*Philip Yancey*

Discerning God's Voice

Contemplation

In Isaiah God makes an incredible promise to his people: "Your own ears will hear him. Right behind you a voice will say, 'This is the way you should go'" (Isaiah 30:21). Wouldn't it be amazing if we heard God this clearly?

Learning to hear and recognize God's voice is something I've wrestled with since I was a girl. People talk about a relationship with Jesus, and that implies communication: talking and listening. But what does that mean? How do I live that out? I studied the Scriptures and asked people, "*How* do you hear from God?" And one of the things I heard over and over is that many experience God's voice as a thought that's a little brighter than most.

We must always be careful to maintain an attitude of humility as we try to discern God's voice. Scripture should be the foundation and filter for anything God says. If what we think God is telling us doesn't line up with God's Word, then we know it isn't from him. In addition, we should look for a sense of peace. In Philippians 4:7 Paul wrote that God's peace will guard our hearts and minds. We also need to ask whether what we heard was blanketed in love. A bitter, cutting voice is not from God.

Often God is diligently and persistently communicating to us in various ways; I call these messages "sacred echoes." For example, a sacred echo can be a moment when we're reading the Bible, and it comes alive. Then we go to church, and the pastor is teaching on that same story or passage. Later that week we go to lunch with friends, and that same topic pops up in the conversation. Finally, we realize that maybe God is at work, trying to get our attention! God *is* speaking to us through the Holy Spirit as Isaiah promised. As we're attentive to life with a listening spirit, we'll recognize the sacred echoes in our lives.

—*Margaret Feinberg*

A chief attribute of contemplation is an open heart. When I walk into my day saying yes to God and to the world God has created, an act as mundane as riding the train to work is transformed into deep and joyous prayer.

—**Vinita Hampton Wright**

I'll ask God for wisdom regarding next steps to take. I might write some ideas. Sometimes this musing will lead to plans. Other times my period of contemplation is simply a time of letting go of all outcomes and experiencing the freedom God wants to give.

—*John Ortberg*

There's one thing I hope I never get over as long as I live: that the awesome Creator of the universe is choosing to speak to me—not just once in a blue moon, but most of the time!

—*Nancy Beach*

> I think sometimes it takes more passion to be truly engaged with God all day than to spend an hour of quiet time in the morning.
>
> —*Priscilla Shirer*

Planting a garden and caring for it is a spiritual act of faith for me.

—Cindy Crosby

Faith isn't really about what we can muster up, power through, or pretend we understand. No, faith isn't really about us at all. It's about who we place it in.

—Holley Gerth

It is the fear of God that puts all other fears in proper perspective.

—Ruth Bell Graham

Just as darkness is the womb of being, so it is the beginning of faith.

—*Sally Morgenthaler*

Fasting

> *Fasting is a critical discipline for the life of the spirit—through fasting we respond in obedience to God's urgings, we come to know ourselves (and our sins) more fully, and we turn to God in complete reliance as we seek his will in difficult situations.*
>
> —Richard J. Foster

Fasting

Disciplining our bodies and stilling our minds through fasting cause something mysterious and beyond description to take place. It brings mental clarity and reminds us how vulnerable and dependent we are on God, as we listen closely to him.

—*Alise Barrymore*

Fasting

As we engage in fasting and experience hunger pangs both literal and figurative, it's helpful to ask ourselves, What am I truly hungering for? *It might not be chocolate after all.*

—*Helen Lee*

The meaning of hunger—indeed, of all desire—is to point us to God.

—Ben Patterson

> *Nothing enables us to forgive like knowing in our hearts that we have been forgiven.*
>
> —*Lewis B. Smedes*

> Self-forgiveness is a long, arduous journey. But when we finally live in its truth, new life awaits. Chains are broken. Dependence, gratitude, and grace permeate our hearts and redefine who we are.
>
> —Suanne Camfield

Scripture calls us to forgive—and to pray for those who hurt us. Although emotionally it can feel impossible, perhaps it's in those difficult prayers that the miracle of true forgiveness begins.

—**Sherryl Stone**

Forgiveness is reserved for deep, serious hurts that result from the evil actions of others. We can overlook *a friend forgetting to give us a ride; we must* forgive *the friend who lies to us.*

—Vinita Hampton Wright

Naturally our calling to live and breathe thanksgiving is high—so high as to be humanly impossible. . . . We will have moments when a pure and complete thanksgiving floods our souls, but most days we'll live in hope.

—*Mark Galli*

Gratitude changes our focus from our neighbors to God. From what we don't have to what God has done. From our desires to our blessings.

—*Amy Simpson*

> I have two daily habits that plant the seeds of gratitude in my life. I don't get out of bed until I've told God what I'm grateful for, and every night I don't close my eyes until I thank God for what he's done that day.
>
> —*Sally Clarkson*

> *Let your roots grow down into him, and let your lives be built on him. Then your faith will grow strong in the truth you were taught, and you will overflow with thankfulness.*
>
> —*Colossians 2:7*

Inviting In, Reaching Out

Hospitality

"Love each other with genuine affection, and take delight in honoring each other. Never be lazy, but work hard and serve the Lord enthusiastically. Rejoice in our confident hope. Be patient in trouble, and keep praying. When God's people are in need, be ready to help them. Always be eager to practice hospitality."

Love, devotion, enthusiasm, rejoicing, patience, eagerness: these are the virtues that Paul calls us to in Romans 12:10–13. They weave together to create a portrait of the demeanor that should characterize our lives. Hospitality is an essential part of this picture. It's a way of living transparently in our interactions with others as we reveal the things we hope for, are afflicted with, and have spiritual fervor for, and practice those things with joy, patience, and faithfulness. It's about serving others with honor and loving others above ourselves. It's creating a safe place for people to come and share life with you. And one hopes that sharing our real lives with others will draw them closer to Christ.

How powerfully would we influence our neighborhood, apartment building, book club, or workout class if we devoted ourselves to them in love, being generous with our time and things? Would the world look at Christians differently? God has called us to be hospitable and to live transparently—continually inviting people into our homes and our lives—so that others might feel welcomed into a spiritual family with God the Father.

—*Lindsey Learn*

What seems so simple—for example, sharing a peanut butter sandwich and being with somebody—can give that person hope at just the right time.

—*Michele Hershberger*

Laughter and good company can be much more nourishing than a fancy meal!

—*Greg Asimakoupoulos*

> In hospitality we can invite others in, even into our hurts, insecurities, and shortcomings as we live within and express our reliance upon God's generous grace for all our not-good-enoughs.
>
> —*Holley Gerth*

Unless I connect with God's love for me, and see myself being hosted by God, I have little to give others.

—Michele Hershberger

> *The word* justice *in the original Greek and Hebrew (dikaio-sune; tsedhaqah) is actually the same word that is also often translated as* righteousness. *Justice, in other words, means making all that is wrong in our world right.*
>
> —Helen Lee

> *Justice isn't a "project" for the church; it's a passion of God. As our congregations grow to understand that God is just and that God seeks justice, we can respond with action.*
>
> —Mark Labberton

Meaningful action begins with transforming our despair about injustice into imaginative solutions. It begins with the question, What am I going to do about it? *Then, with finding the courage to take that first small step.*

—Karen Keen

Who in our lives are we ignoring and forgetting? Who needs justice? On the streets where we live, at the schools our kids attend, at the places we work—who among us is desperately in need of an advocate?

—*Caryn Rivadeneira*

> *Lay down your need to pontificate, prognosticate, or otherwise be the expert, and invite Jesus to mentor you. Receiving mentoring from Jesus, and from him through others, is an antidote to grandiosity.*
>
> —*Adele Ahlberg Calhoun*

What I'd like to suggest to potential mentors is this: Forget the titles. Forget the label. Forget the role even. But please *do this one thing: love the women in your life. Actually care.*

—Mindy Caliguire

Paul never said, "I am making you mature." Rather, he said Christ needs to be "fully developed" in our lives (Galatians 4:19). That's the Holy Spirit's work; as mentors, we seek to be colaborers with God.

—Roberta Hestenes

> *A mentor has accomplished great good when she has taught the individual the joy of accomplishment.*
>
> —*Fred Smith*

> *As we publicly identify ourselves with Christ, we ought to be aware of the temptation to "use" our faith for selfish gain. As we witness publicly of our faith, we must rely on God to help us develop and maintain pure motives for doing so.*
>
> —*Caryn Rivadeneira*

> God's kingdom is spread by the same method it's been spread for two thousand years: through Christ-followers who reach beyond their circle of Christian friends, develop meaningful relationships, and bring people to Christ—one life at a time.
>
> —John Ortberg

> *Evangelism is more than just words; it is also our actions. And we do those good deeds in the name of Christ, no matter what the cost.*
>
> —Linda Taylor

I can relate a bit to the demon-possessed man Jesus healed in Mark 5. This man wanted to follow him to the ends of the earth—but Jesus told him instead to go back to his village and share the Good News.

—***Heather Holleman***

Praying Scripture

Many years ago several young college students sat around the old oak table in Ruth Bell Graham's kitchen, listening to her stories. We were lonely and homesick. College life had been rougher than expected. Ruth talked to us frankly about bouts of loneliness and discouragement she'd battled during her life—she emphasized one particular incident that had laid her low.

"When I was thirteen," she said, "my parents, missionaries in China, enrolled me in boarding school in what is now Pyongyang, North Korea. It was a difficult parting, and on my last night home, I earnestly prayed that I would die." Ruth didn't die, but arriving in Korea, she succumbed to severe homesickness. Every night she buried her head in her pillow and cried herself to sleep. Finally in desperation, she went to her sister, Rosa, also enrolled at Pyongyang.

"I don't know what to tell you to do," Rosa replied bluntly, "unless you take some verse and put your own name in it. See if that helps."

Ruth told us how she then picked up her King James Bible and turned to a favorite chapter, Isaiah 53, and put her name in it: "He was wounded for Ruth's transgressions, he was bruised for Ruth's iniquities: the chastisement of Ruth's peace was upon him; and with his stripes Ruth is healed" (Isaiah 53:5).

"I claimed that verse and knew then," Ruth told us, "that I would make it."

Ruth went on to explain her habit of praying Scripture—of repeating to God the words of his promises and truths. This habit of personalizing Scripture passages and speaking them back to God in prayer formed an essential pattern in her spiritual life. "God loves to be reminded of his promises," Ruth told us. "He never rebukes us for asking too much."

—*Robert J. Morgan*

> We labor hard in our spiritual lives and in our prayer requests, but perhaps what we ultimately need at times is simply to be quiet and rest in God's presence. These times of rest, quietness, and trust should play a key part in our persistent prayers.
>
> —Patricia Raybon

Each time we pray, we trust him as the One who holds the answers—whatever they might be—to our prayers.

—Becky Tirabassi

Interceding for others is a way of loving them, deeply and meaningfully. This gift takes on real meaning when I consider that one day I will likely have my own turn as the paralytic on the stretcher. I will covet and rely on the prayers of others.

—Tracy Balzer

Prayer

God wants us to come to him with integrity, not to present a nice front and keep the real stuff—pain, guilt, frustration, loneliness, confusion—hidden away. In prayer he invites us, like the psalmists, to come to him with our honest thoughts and feelings.

—**Heather Gemmen Wilson**

Preacher, homemaker, cheesemaker—whatever our vocations, we are here for a reason. God's kingdom is at hand, breaking in, offering the job opportunity of a lifetime. We get to help him make shalom. Anything less is beneath our dignity.

—**Carolyn Arends**

Reconciliation

For God was in Christ, reconciling the world to himself, no longer counting people's sins against them. And he gave us this wonderful message of reconciliation. So we are Christ's ambassadors; God is making his appeal through us.

—*2 Corinthians 5:19-20*

If Francis of Assisi were to speak to us today, I can imagine him raising the topic of peacemaking and wondering why many modern Christians have so little to say about it. I can imagine him asking us, "Ought this not be an essential piece of your faith?"

—*Gordon MacDonald*

To love our neighbor as ourselves is a profound undertaking because it requires a respect and consideration that doesn't come naturally. It begins with submission: giving up my rights to meet another's needs.

—**Holly Vicente Robaina**

A God-Paced Life

Our lives are often jam-packed with responsibilities, commitments, relationships, and ministries. Yet is a busy, hectic, overscheduled, and underrested life really what God has in mind for us?

Rather than living at the frenetic pace championed by our culture (and sometimes also by our churches), we are called to live a God-paced life. A life that models his priorities; that breathes his values; that allows space and time for spiritual refreshment, emotional enjoyment, and physical rest.

Psalm 23 paints a picture of what a God-paced life can be like. When the Lord is our Shepherd, we have everything we need, so we don't have to worry. In that psalm God tells me to "rest in green meadows" and that he "leads me beside peaceful streams" and "renews my strength." Leading a God-paced life means allowing the Lord to be our guide so that we can go on the right paths that honor his name.

We can take our schedules, commitments, and relational demands before God and sincerely ask, *Lord, what is it you want me to focus on? How best can I take time to rest?*

We can say to him (and this can be difficult), *Shepherd, give me the courage to give up those things that prevent me from living a God-paced life.*

Rather than always feeling compelled to do more—even doing more good things, such as ministry to others—we can seek to honor God by aiming to discover and focus on the specific things he's called us to, and letting go of all the rest. Ephesians 2:10 reminds us that God created us "in Christ Jesus, so we can do the good things he planned for us long ago." We seek to do what God has planned for us, to walk on the path he has for us, and to do it at the pace he has for us. As we abide in Christ and allow him to guide us in what we do, we're free to turn away from the "do-everything" pace of our culture and live a truly God-paced life.

—Cynthia Heald

The way into Christian Sabbath observance isn't so much about rules as orientation: away from the busyness of the week and toward the Creator who rested. In this we may find a true sense of Shabbat shalom, *Sabbath peace.*

—*Lauren F. Winner*

Choosing rest means consciously overlooking the things that working women everywhere feel obliged to fix or guilty about not fixing: crumb-covered floors, piles of snow, foody dishes, overflowing inboxes, ringing phones.

—Jonalyn Fincher

When we don't cram every minute with activity, it helps us see more clearly what matters. Sabbath is a time set apart to "let the message about Christ, in all its richness, fill your lives" (Colossians 3:16).

—*Amie Hollmann*

> *Rest is more than having down time, and it's more than obeying the fourth commandment. God doesn't want us to toe the line; he wants our full heart—which means he calls us to rest in him* continually, *not just on Sunday afternoons.*
>
> —Heather Gemmen Wilson

I've learned that if you volunteer to feel good, you'll work a few shifts, then give it up. The work isn't easy—not everyone we serve is grateful. There are hard days that shatter our lofty ideals about fighting hunger.

—*Cindy Crosby*

Service

> *Like Christ, we must strive to live in a way that links humility with the attitudes and actions of servanthood.*
>
> —*Timothy Keller*

The thought of being hidden—unnoticed and overlooked—slays us. Let's be honest: it can be very hard to serve when our service goes unnoticed.

—*Kevin A. Miller*

> *When you find yourself touched on an emotional level—when you sense God is tugging on your heart or convicting you, I encourage you to say yes to God.*
>
> —Kay Warren

> *To be a faithful creature of God is to learn something of God's rhythm of silence and sound and silence, to respect and trust it, and then to imitate God by speaking and listening from the context that is as old as the world.*
>
> —**Cornelius Plantinga, Jr.**

Have a pen and pad of paper nearby as you settle in your quiet spot, then simply write every distracting thought that comes into your head. By writing them down, you can be assured that all of those important items will not be forgotten.

—*Tracy Balzer*

> *The darkness of mystery and silence opens up whole new vistas for us, and gives us the ears to hear the whisper.*
>
> —*Mark Galli*

Silence

Prayer is often supplication, a heart begging for comfort. Prayer is often praise, lifted up to God. In using words, we have a clear sense of what we want to accomplish. But silence before God is also a form of prayer.

—*Catherine Bowler*

> *The curious truth is that the discipline of simplicity opens us to possibility, not scarcity. Greed keeps us stuck and selfishly turned inward. Simplicity is a constant yes to the call of the larger life of generosity.*
>
> —Amie Hollmann

> *True, deep-rooted simplicity is about a lot more than just uncluttering our closets; it's a practice of uncluttering our souls. It's a way of life that makes choices and sets boundaries so our souls have space to rest in God.*
>
> —*Ginger Kolbaba*

Living in simplicity involves choosing to wait, to abide, and to rest. Instead of rushing everywhere, a woman of simplicity is wise in what she says yes to, so she's not preoccupied, stressed, and always in turmoil.

—Cynthia Heald

> Our pace may be sometimes slow, sometimes quick. But that pace can become deliberate and "simple" when our perspective is fixed on the "one thing worth being concerned about" (Luke 10:42): ordering our life around Christ.
>
> —*Nicole Unice*

Solitude teaches us to live in the presence of God so that we can be with people in a way that helps them rather than manipulates them.

—*Richard J. Foster*

What might happen, in the church and in our very souls, if every Christian took a two-hour nature walk each weekend, without speaking? Or if we observed a day of being alone? How might we better learn to love God and humanity?

—Philip Yancey

Solitude doesn't have to be an agonizing forty days in a desert or a lonely weekend at a silent retreat. Sometimes it can simply mean being a few steps from our waiting friends while we seek God.
—*Caryn Rivadeneira*

> *Through the practice of solitude, we can reconnect with God one on one. Solitude builds faith by forcing us to depend on God for relationship—and for the truth about life.*
>
> —*Amy Simpson*

Caring for Creation

When we take action to protect the earth God gave us, we also serve the poor, the importance of which is discussed throughout the Bible. Environmental decay results in dirty air, toxic water, soil erosion, and the depletion of species, all of which impact poor people first and hardest.

And then there's the simple command God gave. In Genesis 1, the refrain "it was good" follows God's creation of sunlight and stars, willow trees and orchids, red-winged blackbirds and white-tailed deer. What God created is a gift to us, and in verse 15 he commands us to take care of it. The Fall made that directive more difficult, but there's been no release from this caretaking mandate.

Romans 8:19–22 tells us creation groans and waits to be liberated from its bondage to decay, and Hosea 4:3 paints the picture of the direct impact our sins have on creation: "That is why your land is in mourning, and everyone is wasting away. Even the wild animals, the birds of the sky, and the fish of the sea are disappearing."

. . . Christians can, and perhaps should, be at the forefront of efforts to preserve God's creation. Perhaps just as Jesus' resurrected body was recognizable but new, the new heaven and new earth promised to us (2 Peter 3:13) is from the template of this earth we now know.

So recycle! And do it with your children, teaching the next generation to value God's creation along the way. Turn off the lights when you leave a room. Consider buying a fuel-efficient car. Research and get involved in ways that support environmental causes and are in line with biblical values. And the next time you witness a sight that makes your heart come alive, that renews your passion, that whispers to you of the presence of a good God—remember that God created what you're looking at in order for you to have just such a response.

—Nancy Ortberg

Stewardship

Rather than possessiveness, stewardship requires gratitude. Rather than a sense of entitlement, God calls us to responsibility. How selfish we are to think God's gifts are ours to do with as we please—or to ignore.

—**Amy Simpson**

Stewardship reminds us, "The earth is the Lord's and everything in it" (Psalm 24:1). It tells us, Everything I have is on loan from God, so being careful with his stuff shows him respect.

—Holly Vicente Robaina

> *Every dollar we spend is a stewardship decision. I used to think only big purchases mattered. Now I think that whether or not I go out to lunch is, in some ways, a kingdom decision.*
>
> —*Kara Powell*

There are always people who need something we steward for God: time, money, gifts, talents, cars, airline miles, hotel credits, houses, and on. Will we share? Will we invite God to use these resources for his purposes, not ours?

—*Adele Ahlberg Calhoun*

Submission doesn't mean that you never speak up. But it does mean you resist speaking against *a person, and you treat him or her with respect. You interact with the person in a way that's blameless.*

—*Nancy Guthrie*

> *Once we seek what God has in mind for us, then he begins to make us a vessel fit for glory. But we must be pliable. As the Potter works the clay, he continually wets it. If he doesn't, it gets dry and becomes a misshapen lump, good for nothing.*
>
> —Jill Briscoe

Submission, often misunderstood as weakness, actually requires a strength and determination. We live with a sense that God requires something of us—and we live determined to follow the instructions God gives us.

—Kelli B. Trujillo

> When we're in a healthy relationship with God, we know God's character. We recognize his voice. We may not understand why God calls us to do or not do certain things, but we choose to listen. . . . We choose to trust him—and to obey.
>
> —*Heather Gemmen Wilson*

> *Authentic worship encompasses both friendship with God and fear of God. It is the proper response when a holy God extends to flawed human beings an invitation to intimacy.*
> —**Philip Yancey**

> "The heavens proclaim the glory of God" (Psalm 19:1). This is how to pay tribute to God: pay attention to his glory everywhere. Worship is the life-song of a soul gazing on God, the witnessing of geese-song gliding up into glory.
>
> —*Ann Voskamp*

> *If we give up our ulterior agendas, we can go in the presence of God ready to receive what God wants to happen. And then God surprises us. There is a splendor in worshiping God—in getting to know God in all his fullness.*
>
> —Marva Dawn

As we focus on God's presence and glory in worship, our hearts are humbled. We're stunned by his greatness and our smallness. Our pride shrinks, his glory shines.

—Jack Hayford

For Further Reflection

For Further Reflection

For Further Reflection

For Further Reflection

For Further Reflection

For Further Reflection

For Further Reflection

For Further Reflection

For Further Reflection

For Further Reflection

Transforming everyday matters into a life that matters every day

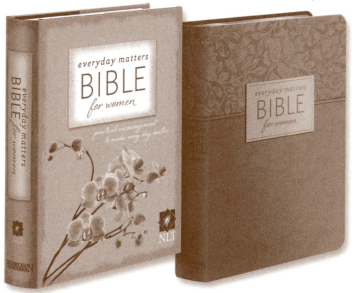

Special Features:

- **EVERYDAY MATTERS:** Two-page articles focus on understanding and practicing a spiritual discipline

- **EVERYDAY PROFILES:** Profiles of twenty-five women in the Bible who experienced many of the same challenges that we face today

- **EVERYDAY REFLECTIONS:** Selections that illustrate how to personalize and apply God's word

- **EVERYDAY Q & A'S:** Short articles delve into difficult topics and offer practical help

Created in partnership with *Today's Christian Woman*, the **Everyday Matters Bible for Women** is designed to bring a deeper sense of meaning into your everyday life.

The contemporary New Living Translation® and over 300 reflections, articles, and meditations from today's foremost Christian writers combine to help you develop spiritual practices that will make your life richer, not harder.

Available wherever Christian books are sold

 facebook.com/EverydayMattersBible